The Things I Didn't Share...

Archi Verma

Copyright © Archi Verma
All Rights Reserved.

This book has been self-published with all reasonable efforts taken to make the material error-free by the author. No part of this book shall be used, reproduced in any manner whatsoever without written permission from the author, except in the case of brief quotations embodied in critical articles and reviews.

The Author of this book is solely responsible and liable for its content including but not limited to the views, representations, descriptions, statements, information, opinions, and references ["Content"]. The Content of this book shall not constitute or be construed or deemed to reflect the opinion or expression of the Publisher or Editor. Neither the Publisher nor Editor endorse or approve the Content of this book or guarantee the reliability, accuracy, or completeness of the Content published herein and do not make any representations or warranties of any kind, express or implied, including but not limited to the implied warranties of merchantability, fitness for a particular purpose.

The Publisher and Editor shall not be liable whatsoever...

Made with ❤ on the BookLeaf Publishing Platform
www.bookleafpub.in
www.bookleafpub.com

Dedication

This book is dedicated to myself. To my 1 a.m. wandering thoughts that never let me sleep. To my self-doubts that always instigated my inner confidence. To my inner battles that make me question my own existence. To the never-ending debate between my heart and mind. And most importantly, to my brother, whose skepticism challenged me and, in doing so, became an unexpected source of motivation, pushing me to complete this. Thanks for always trusting me!

Preface

This is a collection of poetry that is meant to reflect the emotions and thoughts that have made me who I am over the years...such late-night speculations, doubt, realizations that are so quiet and often unnoticed in the quick pace of life. While writing these poems, I explored the themes of self-doubt, solitude, and the never-ending fight between heart and mind. I write this book for the sake of giving voice to the emotions some of us fail to express. I have used poetry to understand the world around me, my way of navigating the quiet and the loud moments as well. I hope that here, you will find within these words an echo of yourself, some thought or feeling that touches you and some healing as well. Thanks for picking up this book-an experience to be shared with me.

Acknowledgements

I would like to express my deepest gratitude to everyone who supported me throughout the writing of this book. To my brother, *Ayush Bhaiya* thank you for always being by my side, this could not have been possible without your constant encouragement. To Mom and Dad, who understood my passion, thank you for your unwavering encouragement and belief in me, even during the most challenging moments. A special thanks to my musketeers also, who kept awake whole night listening to my over - thinking and made me believe that I could do it. Thank you so much, *Kaydee* this book would not have been possible without your support.

Lastly, to the readers—thank you for choosing this book and for sharing in the journey I've set out to tell. It is your curiosity and passion that make this all worthwhile.

With all my gratitude,

-Archi Verma

1. More or Meaningful?

We spring up with the sun, we labor, we grind.
We are bound to the clock, enslaved by time.
Counting pennies, chasing pay,
yet still, we are hungry for more.
There is a house, built tall—warm and whole,
yet a mansion on a golden street is still the goal.
A table is before us with plenty so grand,
but a delicacy for the palate is still in demand.

Voices surround, laughter swirls,
yet still, solitude settles in our hearts.
A world with the screens so wide
- each attention-seeker calling for followers to confide in.
But why, oh why, is enough not enough?
Why is there still a "more" that calls us to their bluff?

We run, we run.
We are never to arrive,
and we forget to live for the moments that make us alive.
Did you ever pause and lay on the grass,
allowing the night to tell you stories through the stars?
Each twinkle up above is a whisper, a song, reminding us
gently
 – we belonged all along.

Try feeding a stray and watch his tail dance;
No number of likes can compare to that glance.
A villa will never compare to a home that breathes,
where love resides and warmth weaves through its
seams.
Step into the rain, let it kiss your face,
Feel the sky sink deep in its soft embrace.

Let the earth hum songs,
travelling through your feet to hug the trees,
to hear their heartbeat.
Smile at a stranger and hold a hand;
but lose yourself in the art of living
—not what is demanding.

Because for all that we chase,
for all that we crave,
there is nothing left but dust
when we go beyond the grave.
So, find abundance in the little things,
the laughter, the sun, the song life sings.
Because after all, one day when you close the door,
no wealth will matter if you don't have to need more.

2. Art Of Letting Go

I was born with fire flowing through my veins,
And a heart that never learned to wait.
If I wanted something, I had to take it,
Regardless if it be love, or dreams, or fate.
For countless nights, and more days than I could ever count,

I wrote my name on every inch of page.
Top of the class, at the very top,
Taking risks for a world of dreams I had forged.
The wind howled by as I rode the road,
The bicycle I wanted, the love I rolled,
With arms stretched open, I took it all,

Without fear to tumble, or fall and or crawl.
Then the storm arrived and broke me,
The universe, I created, with my reckless heart.
The love I thought would never end,
or wanted to completely, decided to bend.
The job, I dreamed, oh the pure light,
Grabs hold of the divine and disappears from sight.

Oh how I burned, oh how I tried
For the gold stars of my life and never replied.

I begged the past to continue with me,
To stitch up my wounds, and clothed me free.
And someone said in the middle of my hurt,
"The more you hold, the more you hurt."

Perhaps the love was never suppose to last,
Or perhaps it never meant some job would take so many
past.
Therefore, I relinquished- I released everything.
I stood open, facing the flow.
No constraints, no darkness, no bad hands,
Just trust in time's unfolding plans.

Life is transitory. Moment leave us quickly.
Not all we love is intended to be eternal.
And if old memories cause me pain,
I launch them like a bird unbound.
For living is not a prize to earn,

Nor battles to be engaging in chasing your lucky role.
Living is waiting, it's loss, it's learning very slowly and
- To breathe, to fracture, to ascend, to evolve.

3. Hope

For one, many times there will be fading rainbow colors.
People will reveal their true, darker shades,
and one's truth may become twisted,
turning innocent bliss into deceiving lies.

We often live one way while, deep inside, we long for
another
—longing, even, for death...
But hold on, dear soul, don't let go.
For happiness, the Almighty, will soon rise into the air
and take you into her embrace.

At once, success will raise you up again.
You will spread your wings once more,
no longer bound by what once held you back.
You shall live life on your own terms
—no more adapting, no more begging anyone to stay
behind.

Again, you will see clearly,
resurrecting the respect once lost along the way.
No more tears. No more pain.
A moment will come when you decide to break the
chain.

This is the moment to rise, to gather your shine, and choose to fight.

The world may still urge you to give up, but don't forget to try.

For in that very minute, you will soar like an eagle, bathed in the sunlight above, flying freely among the clouds.

4. Love Within Us

How can Love be a lifelong pursuit?
A thirsty sensation that lasts forever,
a dream that I can't seem to forget?
Is it true that Love is only present in the perfect person's
arms?
A man with a heart to protect? (Partner, too)!

Maybe not, since Love lacks a suitable form of
expression.
The feeling is everlasting, unrestricted, and illimitable.
Love is alive within me,
Smiles enveloping infants, pure joy,
In silent prayer to ease a pained soul,
In all positions, every word, each phrase.
I'm the radiance, the vitality, and the brightness.

Is the love of another person truly necessary?
No, as the love of no one else is ingrained in me.
Similar to a wandering bee, seeking your embrace,
The giver, the keeper, or tender, tender grace is me.

My love is unrestricted, it runs freely without any
constraints.
Have you ever experienced a heartbreak or loss due to

love?
If so, what happened?
It may not be as much an accident as it is a curse.
But a blessing in the form of lessons, too.
With every tear, a lesson learned; with every stumble,
strength regained
Stand up straight, you're tall.
Stronger, braver, wiser than before,
A warrior of compassion, with an open portal.

Not needing anything more, yet no longer seeking,
You have become the Love that everyone else wants..
Not a victim of fate, nor repressed by past traumas,
Nevertheless, a person who instilled love is now free.

Being unloved isn't a complex process,
A sacred space, a chance to recover.
The love that is born within your soul,
Such a wide-ranging love can bring you whole....?
From the river to the sky, your presence is felt.

The never-ending love that will endure.
It's unnecessary to seek love from someone else.
However,
It flows with a never-ending tide within you.
An affection that transcends time and place,
An affectionate sentiment that fills any empty space.

It's just the universe trying to show you this,
You are Love incarnate, wild and unrefined, yet pure in
its essence.
The fear dissipates once you grasp the reality.
Love is not a result of your discovery or deceit.

That's something you are, that gives back.
A beacon of light that will endure..
Escape from searching, release the craving,
Your love grows and is released forever.

5. 21- An age to remember

21! A strange age! In a cage, lost.
At times, I yearn for a touch of warmth,
In need of a shoulder, I am.
I dream of having someone to trust,
To be in a safe place where my heart may flourish.

But the flood arrived suddenly and heavily.
Secrets are kept by a world that is cruel.
Judging, grumbling, and never at peace,
The disguise and the mask are synonymous.
Your steps will turn and become distorted,
You're the wolf alone with a shattered heart.

My maxim is to stay calm and be strong-minded.
Enjoy your life, forget the hurt, and move on.
I thought I would find peace amidst the turmoil,
But you still occupy my space, encroaching on all my
desires.
You roam in my head, unwanted, uninvited;
A specter that I do not fully comprehend.

I try to escape, to hide your presence,
But you are in every corner, everywhere.
All I can do is continue thinking.

The reason I despise myself is that I've turned into what I
never thought I would.
I need a switch to turn it off completely,
To quiet the tempest, to no longer feel anything.
I think this fault, this suffering, is mine.

A portion of me sculpted, the rest left to be watched.
For as long as I can remember, there's always been a
place to go.
My hunger for love is endless,
A pure and sincere desire for attachment,
The love that unites two souls in a profound way.
It's like I'm always reaching, trying, and moving. Why?
An infinite hunger for something, living forever.
I've been searching, roaming, in the dark,
For a sensation left behind.
My only expectation was for someone to hear me,
Someone who would give me their hand.

But nevertheless, the silence buzzes with whispers of
suspicion. Why?
Questioning the nature of love.
21, an age that never ends.
A struggle for focus, something I see.
I'm accustomed to this intensity, this strength of pain.
But I want more.

Seeking a cure, fighting toward completeness,
And yet, utterly indifferent and lacking something
definite.
Even though I'm obsessed with this pursuit, I continue.
Why?
I don't know if I'll ever be the same,
In search of someone to be around,
In search of someone to be here.

I fear I might lose a part of myself.
Yet, still, I wait for the hope that,
For real love, for sagacity in the mirror.
At present, my sole purpose is to remain in this place.
21, roaming, meandering, searching for,
The peace I have waited so long for, at the depths of my
mind.

6. A Love That Wasn't

I don't love you anymore!
At least I tell myself that,
When, at one point, I was obsessed with you,
Living in the world you built,
Where love was an illusion,
I had nothing better to do than chase after,

Running until I reached the places
I thought love could go,
Years into chasing it beyond distraction,
into perpetual eventual gratification.
I thought, "This is everything" when I had you,
Your laugh, your touch, your name beside mine.

And even then, there was emptiness lurking behind all
the noise,
Beneath all the silence.
The skies were pink, and the air was purple,
But my life didn't have the colours of a joyous one.
You were everything I could have ever dreamed about,
And yet I still felt incomplete.

I smiled around you,
But happiness never stuck around inside.

You were the sun on my body,
But never the light bright enough to remove my
shadows.
Holding you brought chills over my being,
But never the calm I so desperately wanted.

Your lips brushed against mine,
But your eyes remained dreaming, locked in passion,
Yet they never understood my silent words.
You were the dream I took to hold,
But maybe, just maybe not the dream reality.

It was not you that lacked,
I had no flaws to uncover in your character.
But love is not about perfection.
Love is the base of a feeling deep inside,
A love that comforts rather than dazzles,
A love that feels like home.

And maybe I mistook infatuation for love,
The excitement of wanting,
The sense of belonging beneath my skin.
Because when I let you go,

I discovered something I had never knew
— A happiness that did not exist because of you,
A joy that was inside of me all along.

So I don't love you anymore...
Or perhaps I never really did.

7. Love: Curse or Boon?

Individuals, brave and unaware, venture for love,
leaving everything behind.
Against their family, against their friends,
in defiance of society, they fly for love.

The world curses them, breath by breath,
and yet they choose love for all it is.
Unnoticeable, unappreciated, and still they stand,
through whatever comes.
No matter how hard the red flags are standing,
the lover stands in defeat, clutching a heart in their
hands.

Endless opportunities, the world at their feet,
Love and emotion always leave them vulnerable.
They know only darkness follows, and fleeting joy never
comes as a surprise.
Their short-lived sadnesses do not surprise them.
They drown in tears, but with love, and they gain some,
and are lost.

For it is the fire that burns, but they continue to want
and chase the flame.
For it is each wound of a poison the heart lives to

swallow.
Madness they say, is love as the ultimate call,
a spell, a curse, a good or bad half.
Nevertheless, love will always be involved in each
sadness.

It is the poison that remembers to not heal.
A bittersweet addiction difficult to break,
the price of love—with everything at stake.
They lose themselves in love, desire, and lust emptying
themselves.
Drowning together in love and harmony, seeking
nothing but connection.

Love is flame that engulfs the soul,
Nourishing the heart, but consuming it whole.
It is the tempestuous gale, and the stillness between,
The unseen passion, a space in between.
Love is the question, though it's not clear,
Is it worth it, or to be feared?

For even in madness, love still calls its name,
Deeply rooted it lies, within the depths of our heart
- to claim. Is it a cross, or an exaltation brought near?
Something to question, yet understood is rare.
So we chase it again, despite all that we know,

Ranked with all love has proven,
the best and the lowest below.
A game of hearts, of laughter and pain,
A cross, an exaltation, a purpose and reason for life.

8. Question of Existence

Why do I exist?

For what purpose almighty has made me?

Through the endless echoes within infinite space.

For what great reason was I made?

Was it a fleeting shadow, or was it a divine spark?

Not merely for survival breathing or to rhythmally go to death.

Or thriving through the grind of nine to five,

In a routine with just a mere survival of dreams.

Is life more than this monotonous days,

Of clockwork hours and structured ways,

Or was I made for a bigger cause, To rise, to stumble, to experience it all?

We find ourselves bound by unseen chains,

The doubts, the duties, the scars.

Binding us with ever-tightening ropes,

We all are lost in a cycle of wants and wishes, of loses and gains.

Trying to find pleasure in the gleam of materialistic satisfaction.

Mistaken about the stars that rise up into the night.

Constantly running: fear to desire, Driven by an

unyielding hunger for more.
Is it all, just a finish line to reach?
A life with no meaning, no curves, no bends?
Or on the contrary, it could be the very rush of going
into the great unknown,
The magic of moments, that none can recreate?
It is within the hush of dawn's golden light.

And the quiet pause within which a thinker may dare to
dream.
Above all, within a broken heart's suffering,
It comes to learn through our deepest failures.
It is within the sound of silent laughter,
Within tear-streaked cheeks after silent fights.

In nature's hush, the river softly sings
And we feel that we have proved ourselves so right yet.
Yet I do wonder what is my goal,
The cause of sustaining, a beacon unswerving,
A reason to keep moving on and fighting,
For making a mark for my liberation.

Wait! Have I too been a fleeting shadow?
Chasing desires in hunger's name,
And it seems like whatever I could gather is just the
same.
I ignored the beauty in simpler things.

The chirp of the morning sparrow.
The warmth of hands, honest smiles,
A simple stroll towards brighter days?

Perhaps life is a woven thread,
A series of moments both alive and dead.
Maybe it is not one glorious dream;
It is wonderment that we map out in small bits.
Yet still the question breathes in my ear;
In the stars and morning skies, it does lie.
Why should I exist?

Is the answer esthetic hidden,
then it is in every inhale where the mystery is sylphlike.
Maybe it is not in all those goals we chase,
But in life's slow and holy embrace.
To feel, to fall, to rise again- To savor the lows and
celebrate the highs,
Maybe not as elaborative as it should have been,
But maybe enough for me.
Because it is to live, question, seek, find;
An embrace of loss and love defines you.
So let me breathe and so let me be,
A quiet note in life's vast symphony.

9. Price of Freedom

At sixteen, skies were a delectable passion,
The open yearning for freedom rang along the ties.
To break away from those walls that shut upon me,
To run with the winds unbound and clear,
To do the things, my mother forbade.
To dance with dusk and roam wide-eyed.

No night-time wandering, no moonlit grace.
Longing for a key to my door.
All nights were to be strung with friends and dreams
galore.
Freedom-brazenly, freedom my heart sigh,
The whispered prayer to the open sky.
"I will study hard," whispered my lips,
"And get my work in foreign lands."

But hush, beneath the noble dream,
A silent request-a secret scheme.
Flee the home that caged my flight
And find the dawn in a stranger's light.
Now twenty-one, four years gone by,
And the nights still feel cold.
The city's loud, the people near,
But none to hold me close and dear.

I groaned for freedom and tasted its bland embrace,
An empty plate; a still place.
It was the freedom I had desired all along,
Yet had given to me the sorrow that I most never
imagined.
No arms of friendly greeting to the day,
Comfort was beautiful during sleepless nights.
The street food fills up, but nothing really should be soul
-it lacks warmth to make me whole.

The wind strokes my lonely face now,
But misses absolutely the touch of my mother's grace.
It's mine, my room, my door shut answered
conversations only;
In the dark, free but for a shadow creeping,
Devils prowl where silence weeps.

When you live with friends,
or some who are supposed to be,
Trust does mean inhaling the sweet words,
Sweet smiles conceal sharpest lies,
Serpents draped in friendship's guise.

The home that I had fled from,
which once translated into feeling as being in chains,
Is now still the land of remedies for all suffering.

Perhaps the grass has never been green,
But rather colored by other-lens invested upon.

And now I crave grace behind the bars,
With love the made perfect silence.
Letting me be a child in mother's ward,
Letting me feel all warmth, so pure, so rare.

But freedom stood for the price of quiet,
And the gains I missed kneel in the sky.
The world seems like one great dimension side.
Where hope and fear together hide.
And now I know the deepest-born cry
Never once did beg for freedom,
But for one to be free.

10. The Battle Within

Heart sighed, "This world isn't all that great."
It cried with doubt swirling inside.
But the mind remained indifferent and cold with its
disagreement.
Perhaps the problem is with you! it insinuated.
There is probably no one, nothing, or anything that could
happen that might be good enough for you.

The whispers intensified, biting cruelly, "It's your fault,
pal. It's all there in you."
Recall the last relationship of yours that did not collapse?
Six months? Less? And no longer, right?
Why does each beginning end at a door?
What is so hard about handling other people's problems,
lightening the load of caring, and trusting what follows?

Why do you run when people want any of their wants,
Be it just a simple hug or a gentle touch?
I know it is hard to want something,
But you do not even want the simple things.
Who would want to stay with you?
Your family? Friends? Who calls you?

Ah, but are not your mind and body breaking anymore?

Tired, confused, every morning?
Others manage even way worse than you, but you still
whine, lost in your head.
You have so much, but there you lie wasting away
everything with every breath.
And that is unfair, not only to yourself but also to
existence itself,
to that gift of life from God, lived whose life in silence
and sadness.

But hey, Mind whispered softly, "Maybe you deserve
such an empty feeling."
You are paying for the wrongs of the past, for hidden-
away memories, for old debts to pay off. With this dark'll
thought, Mind became quiet; it ended it all.
A wrist was to take the blame—an errant cry, a final
ember.

But oh, dear one, as you fight, don't let your mind pull
the reins.
Don't trust the darkest thoughts—they aren't the whole
truth of who you are.

11. Flawless

With straight hair and a slim waist,
Fair skin always remains in style.
Curves that conform, and skin so light,
A stunning smile, a shining light.
Is beauty just a moment so brief?

A painted face, such a thief?
Shouldn't be dark, shouldn't be wide,
Shouldn't have scars that we try to hide.
Whose rules are these, this cruel joke,
That beauty is just something to invoke?

A whisper soft, crystal clear is bold,
Even "flawless" holds "flaw" within its fold.
Beauty can't be only skin deep,
It's in the scars and the laughs you keep.
Stretch marks like rivers snake across sand,
Where our stories and journeys expand.

Freckles like sun-kissed flecks on our face.
Like stars in the sky, finding their place.
Curls that twist line in every direction,
Every imperfection holds its reflection.
Brown is steady like earth and so strong,

How then is fairness the song we prolong?

Why do we run from blemishes
as if Nature herself does not embrace each as a gift?
The moon has spots and still rounds out the night,
The sky is deep gray but still gives off light.
Waves crash and foam wild and chaotic,
Yet still enter the shore, so calm and exotic,

Isn't that the way that beauty should be?
So love yourself just as how you are,
You are the moon; you are the star.
Your imperfections are art; your scars a song.
You have been a masterpiece all along.
So love the beauty on the inside;
You are unique and have nothing to hide.
The world may be running for perfection all blind,
But you, my love, are one of a kind.

12. Falling Without a Destination

He looked, I lost—my heart stood still,
Draped in chivalry, Elegance at its peak.
His gaze so bold, yet mesmerizing as a breath,
He felt like a man and a dream at death.
The rhythm of his speech, his call, and his smile,
Felt like home—a comforting shed.

A vibe so beautiful, a phase so right,
Maybe he's the one—my life will be light.
So let's wander through streets I don't know,
Hand holding hand where love has grown.
Let's talk and talk, the dusk to dawn,
Where the laughter lingers when the laughter has gone.

Let you be the Chandler, and I be Monica,
No melancholy, just peace and delight
Kiss like we are whispers lost in the air,
Hug like we made the entire world disappear.
Let's bare our souls, hold nothing back,
Share all of our wounds—and flaws,
I'll be your lap when the world has no kind,
And you be my arms and protector of body and mind.

Be the answer to all my overthinkings,
And I'll give you comfort like my child.
Let's chase the stars, follow the chevrons in flight,
Get too lost in each other in the moonlight.
Let's enjoy watching Netflix, let's snuggle in real tight,
Let's relive romantic stories all night.
And re-watch all bollywood rom-coms.

Where love was perfect, and oh so real.
Let me be your comfort, reliable and true,
You be my fire, wild and new.
Let's live, let's feel, let's risk, and let's try,
With no intentions of goodbye.

But wait to fall don't fall too deep,
For love lost is a promise we keep.
And promises decease, as echoes fade,
Like the sun when lost in the shades.
So, let's dive into the journey of love,
Without the expectation of finding the destination.

13. Chasing Shadows

"You got 89, while she got 91,"
Dad's voice pinched, sharp as a knife.
No praises, no hugs of pride;
just another competition,
just finding another reason to decide.

Work harder they said, go harder,
so I stuffed the dreams into the ground
and played the card.
Enduring long nights, me, ink, and page
in hopes of burying the rage.

With a scored paper in my trembling hands,
I could feel hurt in their eyes,
another unspoken; as they denied a look a sigh,
a nod, for someone else had reached the sky.
That's ok I told myself, no tears tonight;
I'll continue on and find a way to shine so bright .

At twenty-one, I thought that I had me
Then, a job was for me.
 And even in that, the whispers came,
"She makes a considerably more and you're just a name."
A cousin older in the family, wise, and wealthy

I was just another energy.

Is this the life I meant to live?
A runt of the kind where love is never free?
Whatever, just proved a contender,
no matter how hard I climbed,
I just was a tender.
Using their words, I used their paint,

I think I worked through fire,
though storms and then rain.
I sacrificed and dreamed,
both faded and dreams died fast.
However, still, they had no pride.

"She has a home," "He owns a vehicle,"
"What makes it impossible for you to reach that far?"
But I ask, what about the weight I carry?
The sleepless nights, the silent pleas?
I carry the weight by myself, carving paths while making
homes.

Only to find that every move I make,
they push the line back, move the posts,
was it ever mine anyway?
"Am I that small? Am I that weak?"
That life, and pride, I don't dare put ahead of my worth.

Or will I always be compared, a name in the shadows?
For once, just once, let me be free,
to live, to thrive, to just exist as me.
No more fights, no more races, just love without
condition.
Is there a world where I am enough?

Where love is complete and not a struggle?
Where I am seen beyond a number,
Without being thought inadequate
—sorry, just forget that.
Tell me dad, tell me true,
is there a world where I am enough for you?
One where nothing matters, and in its place,

14. Why, God?

They say you are the light that we cling to,
The hidden hand or, the power of good that we can't yet
see.
If you steer the stars, Why is this world still without
your light?
This is not blind anger I am having,
But really, God, why does this hurt exist?

If you are just, if you are real,
Why would you let the tender drown in fear?
A child, of just six months, so small, so new,
Yet she is suffering at the hand of people who have no
good in them.
What does she owe? What is her sin?
For that darkness took her dawn away.

If an order of things exists by way of action and
reaction,
If balance exists, Then why do safe, secure hearts gain no
more than a grain of sand?
Why do the humble prayers fall unheard and unseen,
While those who harm run the earth squeaky clean?
And they bow to you, chant for you,
Fast for you through laughter and shame.

With faith unwavering and pure, without fear,
When they find only silence that is their master.
If you have hands to knit the sky,
Then why do love and hatred compete?
Why must two hearts dread to meet,
While laws say to love is a sin.

Why do we measure a woman's value,
Like gold and silver, coin and soil?
Why does power, cold and stern,
Determine who leads and who must learn?
If love is strong, if love prevails,
Why does hate continue to tip the balance?

If prayers are heard, if wishes come true,
Then why are you still so silent?
I do not curse, I do not deny, I only ask - simply tell me why.
For if justice bends to fate, Is this the world that you create?
For once, just once, let the answers rain,
Is suffering truly ordained?

If punishment is for the past,
Then why do children breathe their last?
I do not wish to test your power,

Nor doubt the stars that burn with power.
I only wonder, I only sigh
- If you exist, then please tell me why.

15. More, More, More

I prepared your favorite meal this evening,
Brimming with love, taken in stride.
But all you said was "could've been better,"
Not one bit of my labor took pride.

You wanted more, despite all of my effort,
More flavor, more spice, more time—the same way,
Perhaps for a moment you could notice,
The love I provided in each word you didn't care to say.
Why does it seem that all of us act so blind,
To the weight of an appreciation word meant,

The heart that does is left behind,
As we pursue more and more as our litmus test.
The grass is green, or so we claim,
Yet in this race for more and more,
We trample hearts, we abuse their flame,

Leaving love and warmth at the door.
How did this bare minimum even start?
Since when did love become a debt?
The hands that do, the arms that receive,
Are somehow measured by how much extra?

Mothers cook our favorite meals—
"Isn't that just what mothers do?"
Fathers work to fund our fanciful plans—
"Well, that's his duty, nothing new."
A partner brings a special and thoughtful gift,
But, it's "obligatory," "what is the intent?"

Tell me, when in the world did love become a task?
When did kindness go away?
And yet, even when hearts grow weary and cold,
When hands cease to give, feet cease to chase,
We say— "We don't even get the bare minimum."
How tragic, how pathetic.

We humans, selfish, empty souls,
Not full, yet never thankful,
Always wanting, always taking,
Forgetting what starts love off right.
So where does appreciation go?
Drifting beneath the burden of "more."
Perhaps someday we will discover
- Love, once strained, will not have the tally.

16. Melancholic Waves

My heart's forging, a constant sad beat,
Dejection keeps hitting hard, a quiet memorial of old
hurts.
People say, Just let it go, forget about it.
But it's not that easy when it's stuck with you.
I need someone to understand how deeply I feel.

We are made to feel things, to love, to cry,
But it feels like I've to hide it all.
Flashback to the simple joy from the past also?
Now it's all covered up by hard stuff.
I wasn't like this, been a crazyhead.

Parties were delightful back in the days,
But under, I felt lost by the glimpse of my father
He's 55, floundering to get by,
Trying to make my dreams be.

Guilt really has me down,
Sadness keeps me up at night.
Happy songs might be on,
But Anuv Jain's music always gets to me.
It snaps me back to reality,
And I see a youthful girl with implicit confidence.

That girl had big dreams,
She really wanted to do well.
Now, she's just a shell of who she was.
Buried beneath my failed dreams.
Everything feels like a continuance agone ,
I can not find who I used to be.

She gave up trying to win a game where no one does,
Going after things that did not count.
Solutions that did not work out, voices in my head,
Now just quiet uncertainties.
This life noway stops,

Moreover, I do not have my musketeers presently.
But then, I am agonized,
Trying to pick up the pieces.
I miss being hopeful,

Loving hard, and not feeling bad.
Now I am just a shadow of my old tone,
Lost and just going through the movements.

17. Embrace the Journey

We run and run and run,
Hurrying to a far-off place.
Eyes on the bright shining prize,
Hearts on what comes at the end.
And yes, ambition paves the way,

 A rage, a will to carry on.
But wait, have you ever seen,
The space between, the in between?
We run fast, far and blind,
Without cherishing the moments back in time.
The glow of sunlight on the road,
The whispers light, the words untold.

Each step a story to be found,
With every breath an insight sound.
Laughter taken, tears we shed,
The scars we earned, the dreams we fed.
For there is magic in journeying,
A moment of gaiety, a love, a prayer.

A stumble, a fall, and rise again,
A glimpse here and there of the true.
What if we could stop, if only for now,

To touch the ground, to breathe, to bow?
To taste the rain, to hear the sound,
Of life's rapture, that rolls all around.

The destination gazes proud,
But it only softly suggests that it can help us make
decisions saying,
"Come, but don't run, for the journey deserves grace".
So walk with wonder, walk with ease;
do not forget your heart needs to seize the paths you
travel
and sights you see, my friend, that is destiny.

18. Fading Flames

It is true that I love you, as you see,
Yet it aches my heart, not just me.
I can't bear to see you leave,
Nor do I know how to do so with another.
Yet sometimes, fear entangles me,
And I have doubts if I should just let it be.

If love was made to wheel,
Then, on what part of my life is the deal?
What amounts to commitment, to abide,
When footprints washed away with the tide?
I have needs and wants that remain untouched,
As my heart gets hot or turns to paste.

These sweet kisses that brought me joy,
Now seem empty as a hollow toy.
What has happened to the love that stays?
Love that was not just a few days?
We talk about love as though it abides,
Yet love seems to wash away like the tides.

Could we just pause for a day?
And just experience the journey of heart a bit slowly.
Forget the press race, forget the road.

Just let love be, in its own abode.
And, I don't trust the hands of those who dare,
When love stops trusting then trust lays bare.
I despise the day I first got to know you,

Not knowing that pain would arrive here as well.
You were the light, the heat, the flicker.
And now there is only a name.
Not soft, not brimming with love's hug,
An echo that bounced off the place.

Once upon a time your words took me away on a nightly
flight,
Now they bounce off cold and dry.
Not full, nor with the trust of a kiss,
A shadow suspended in silent happiness.
Can we begin again, create a whole song?
Mmm, reverse the crack and repair a soul?

Turn the pages, start anew,
Trade the past for something true.
Would you kindly take my hand as slowly,
Or was love left outside the door?
I don't even know you again.
We will go back to where we first began, over the phone.

No hidden reason, and no stupid lies.

Just open hearts and honest sky.
Let us speak, let fear vanish, let us just hold hands for a
while.
Not all love ends in vain, Not everything has to be a
pain.
Some hearts heal, some souls grow.
And maybe love will bloom again.

19. Love: A Conditional Affair

They say that love is unconditional,
But is it really?
Sure, I have heard the claim whispered, sung, or declared,
Yet I have witnessed love come and go in life.
They all will endlessly love me- My mother, my father, my friends and my lover,
But underneath the thoughts and the words,
There is something we sometimes cover.

Because love is never truly free,
 It comes with considerable cost, never verbally.
A price that must be paid, a job to do,
A sacrifice that feeds the flame if you will.
My partner loves me, yes, that's true
But only if I make them feel special, too.
If I cannot, will they have love left to give?

If I am not up to the mark, will love still live?
My father has said, he loves me, my dear,
But I hear expectations call very near.
Be strong, be smart, be great, achieve,
As long as I uphold all the standards he needs.

And if I fall short, if I cannot pay,
Will love come to visit all of the way?

And my mother, oh, her love others say is pure,
Love that is deep, steady, and sure.
But I have seen the favor of my sibling,
I have seen the pride, and her happiness in me
dwindling.
For that child could boast each of her dreams,
While I stood in the middle, like a stone in a stream.

Even the street's creatures - the strays,
with such eyes of kindness and sweetness,
they will wag, they will purr,
but only if I bring them food first.
Belly filled, hand warm, then only love will come.

And now I sit and wonder and stare at the illusion of
love in the air.
If love is always about terms, is it love, or just favour
returns?
A trade in many forms, many pretty words.
Then where is love? To live unrestrained, to take and to
give?
Is kindness love? Or a warmth extinguished?

If love always must take shape on the other's self, then is

it love?
Or can I buy it? Because I have searched on,
I have waited on, a love that lingers despite wrong,
a love that stays when I am.
If love is unfettered and knows no shelter, it is love
nearby.
I often ask, do you exist? Unconditional love probably
does;
I'm not sure, but I certainly hope so.

20. Unheard, Yet Loud

"Why are you this way?" they ask me - over and over again.
"Why can't you live up to what we expect?"
"Why aren't you like your brother?"
The words are like the clap of thunder, and yet I keep silent,
Because I don't know how to say it.

"Why do you always take me for granted?"
"Why don't you have time for our friendships?"
"Why are you so selfish?"
The voices get louder, a chorus of discontent,
And still I stay silent.
Because I don't know how to say it.

I am this way!
Not because I choose to be, but because it is me.
A storm hidden by a placid sky,
A river that runs but never cries.
I want so badly to express, to articulate,
But all of the words vanish before they take flight.

My tears betray what I cannot say.
Do you suppose I do not feel?

That the absence of sound is absence of presence,
absence of experience?
No! My heart aches with the things left unsaid,
With emotions submerged beneath lowered wings.
I want to escape the cage and let it all flow out,

But panic quietens my voice,
and still I am silent.
What if I was sounding like I was trembling?
What if my hurt made you turn away?
What if my truth was hard to hear?
There are so many "what ifs," building higher and higher,
until I feel lost in my silent fire.

Just give me time.
A moment of stillness,
a breath in, a hand, that simply holds,
does not ask me to be someone else,
tries to see the language of silence.
Because while I might not say it,
I am feeling it all, love, sadness, longing, regret.
Each word that I do not say is a world from within,
eloping, asking for someone who listens, even if I am
silent.

21. HIM

And with that, he walked away...
HE—who now appearing perfect, turn out to be
unattainable,
Yet even then had the scent of a love of the impossible.
He garnered my shortcomings, and in turn,

Unmasked to me a plethora of graces hidden within my
soul,
Made me feel beautiful and, for the first time, truly
blessed.
Among the messy hair, faded polish,
Where others saw blemish, he saw beauty.

In that naïve boy, where no one else dared venture,
He offered something so unique, so real,
And I his gaze unapologetically unmasked the love that
nurtured.
He resuscitated a self respect buried so deep,

The feeling of affection too profound, as such loving too
enduring,
But to be granted such a tender and warm form was
freeing.
That lineup of letters "love" hitherto concealed,

presented in such romantic manner, and allured me on
repeat.
How? When? Why?

Before I burst into tears, allow me to demonstrate.
He adored my muscle leans more than my face or even
my skin,
And warmed my grin in a way unlike any other.
He would go to cross whichever corner the earth has to
offer,

If only to understand that my delightful glance is a
treasure more priceless than gold.
In fourteen days, he made me feel as though I was the
most fortunate alive,
As though the grandest universe schemed together for
me to triumph, which deep down led me to my salvation.
Oh, his arms encased me,
Like a warm fort, where I was kept free.
And his eyes, as I spoke endlessly,
Had such beauty, it was like a comforting gaze.

He was not a boy, but a man,
A warrior for my body, for love and us,
He was the dream that I longed to understand.

I would build empires and fight wars if I must,
It all felt like an endless story, a love song.

www.ingramcontent.com/pod-product-compliance
Lightning Source LLC
Chambersburg PA
CBHW070602160726
48003CB00005B/2110